Rose Knows...

All about Crystals

Amalia Stamatelatos

AuthorHouse™
1663 Liberty Drive
Bloomington, IN 47403
www.authorhouse.com
Phone: 833-262-8899

Because of the dynamic nature of the Internet, any web addresses or links contained
in this book may have changed since publication and may no longer be valid. The views
expressed in this work are solely those of the author and do not necessarily reflect the
views of the publisher, and the publisher hereby disclaims any responsibility for them.

Any people depicted in stock imagery provided by Getty Images are models,
and such images are being used for illustrative purposes only.
Certain stock imagery © Getty Images.

This book is printed on acid-free paper.

ISBN: 979-8-8230-0963-8 (sc)
ISBN: 979-8-8230-0962-1 (e)

Library of Congress Control Number: 2023910483

Print information available on the last page.

Published by AuthorHouse 06/13/2023

authorHOUSE®

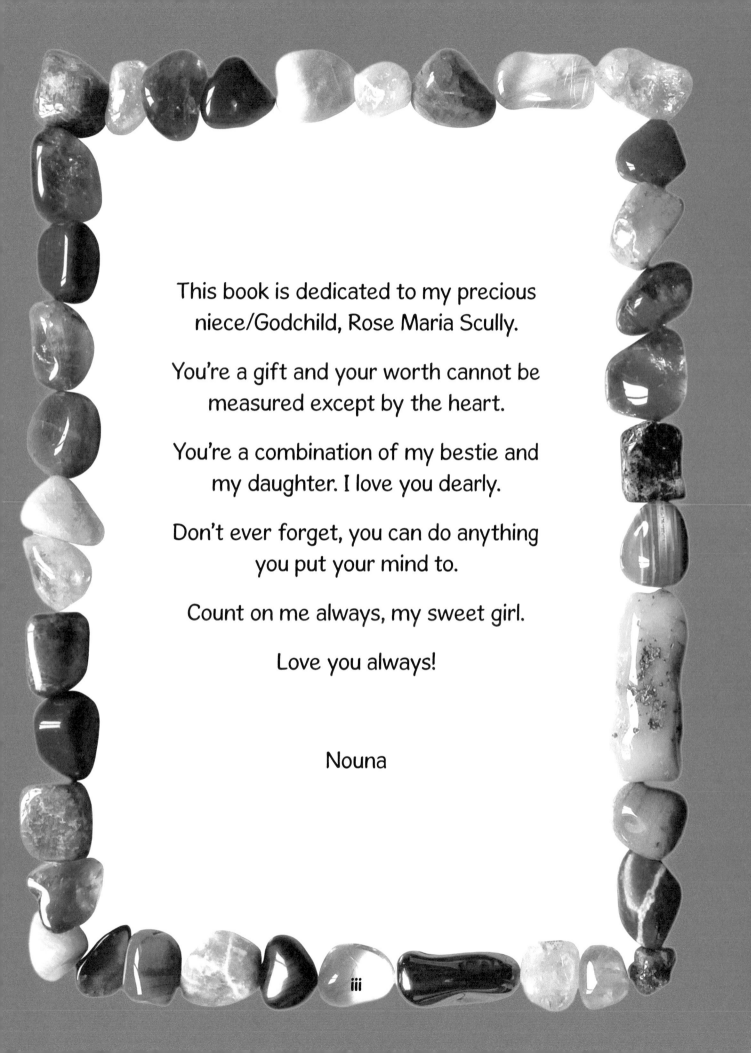

This book is dedicated to my precious niece/Godchild, Rose Maria Scully.

You're a gift and your worth cannot be measured except by the heart.

You're a combination of my bestie and my daughter. I love you dearly.

Don't ever forget, you can do anything you put your mind to.

Count on me always, my sweet girl.

Love you always!

Nouna

Rose Knows...

All about Crystals

Amalia Stamatelatos

Amalia is a Certified Crystal Healer (CCH),
Reiki Master, Certified Animal Reiki,
Certified Chakra Healing practitioner,
and holds a masters in social work (MSW).

1

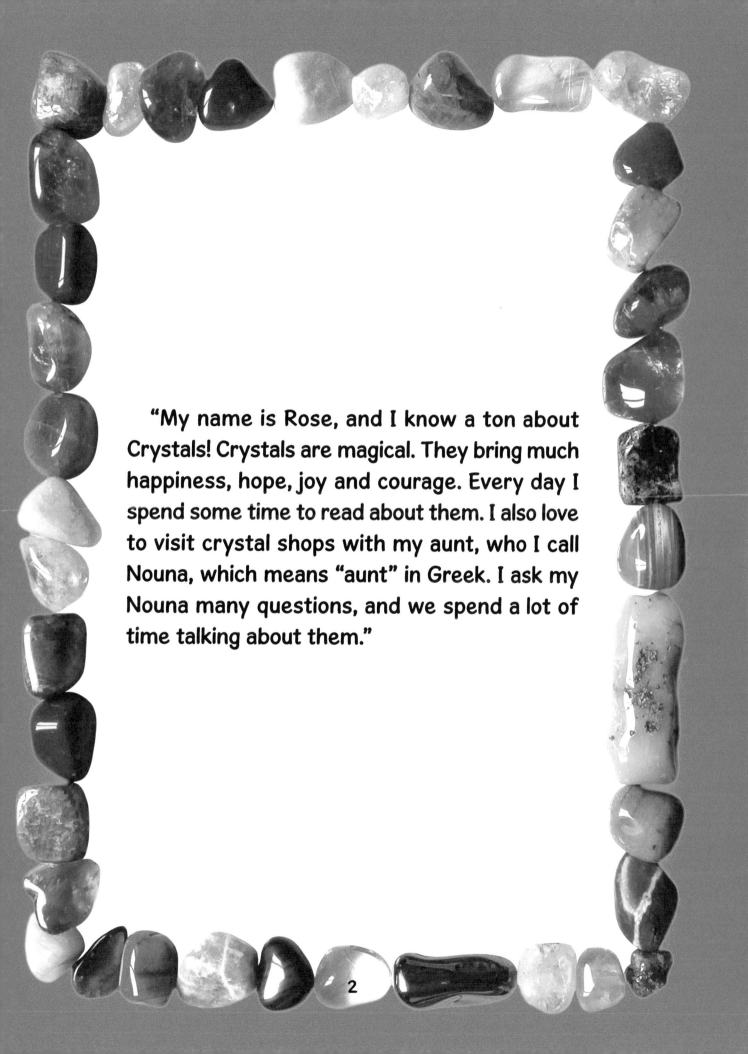

"My name is Rose, and I know a ton about Crystals! Crystals are magical. They bring much happiness, hope, joy and courage. Every day I spend some time to read about them. I also love to visit crystal shops with my aunt, who I call Nouna, which means "aunt" in Greek. I ask my Nouna many questions, and we spend a lot of time talking about them."

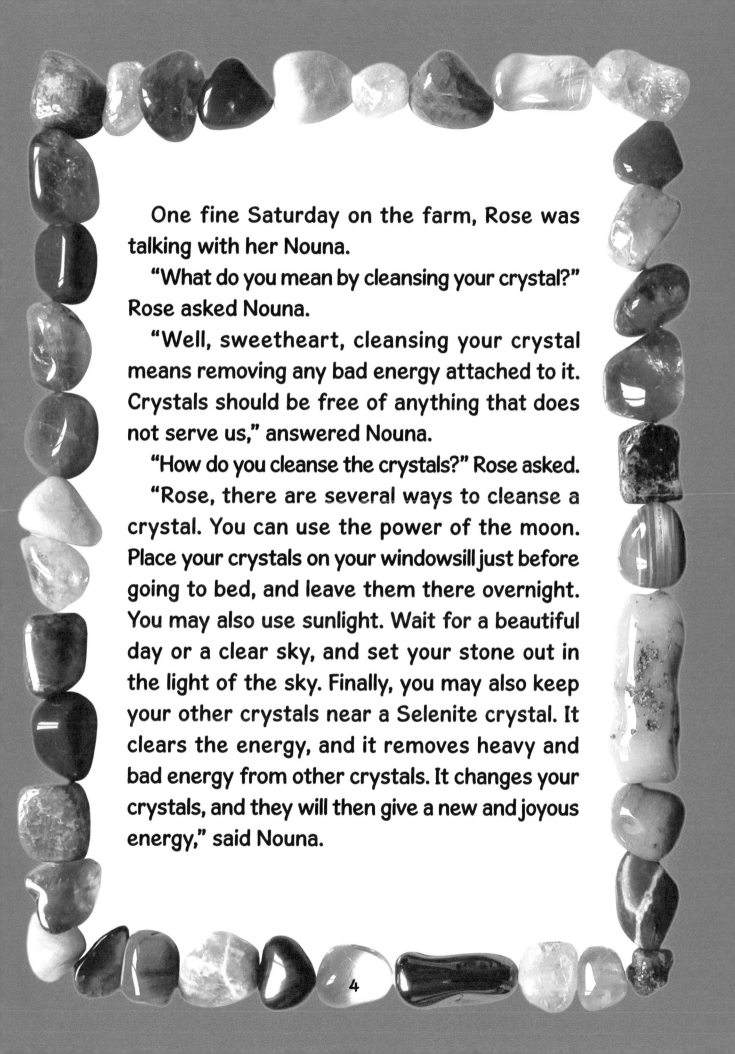

One fine Saturday on the farm, Rose was talking with her Nouna.

"What do you mean by cleansing your crystal?" Rose asked Nouna.

"Well, sweetheart, cleansing your crystal means removing any bad energy attached to it. Crystals should be free of anything that does not serve us," answered Nouna.

"How do you cleanse the crystals?" Rose asked.

"Rose, there are several ways to cleanse a crystal. You can use the power of the moon. Place your crystals on your windowsill just before going to bed, and leave them there overnight. You may also use sunlight. Wait for a beautiful day or a clear sky, and set your stone out in the light of the sky. Finally, you may also keep your other crystals near a Selenite crystal. It clears the energy, and it removes heavy and bad energy from other crystals. It changes your crystals, and they will then give a new and joyous energy," said Nouna.

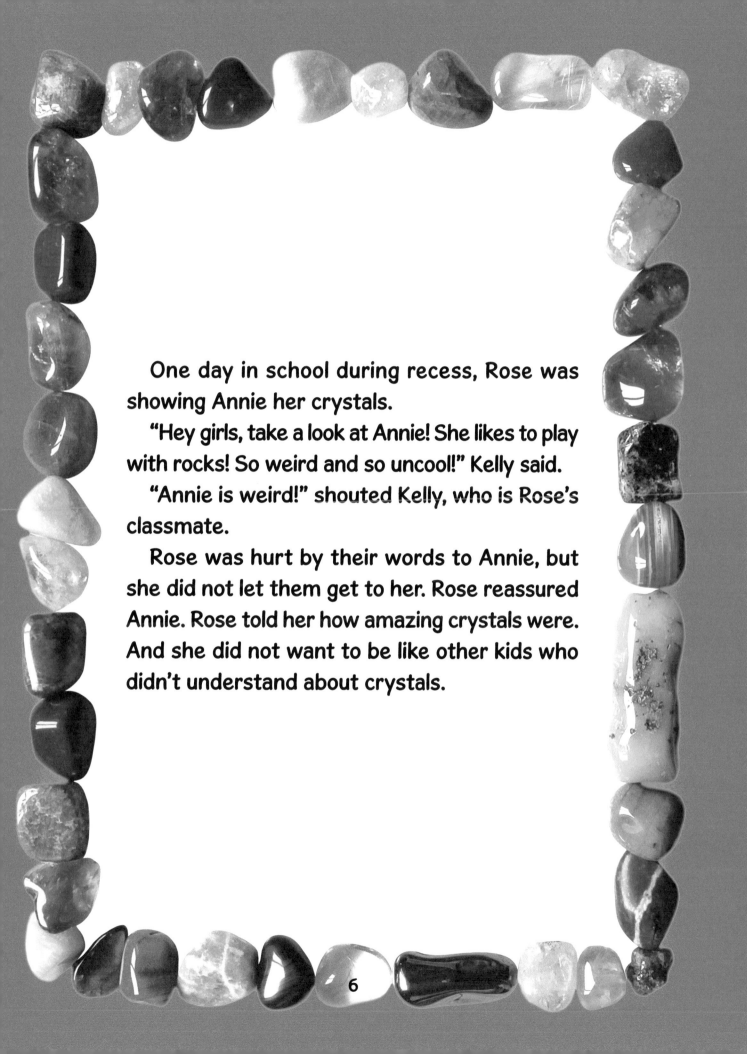

One day in school during recess, Rose was showing Annie her crystals.

"Hey girls, take a look at Annie! She likes to play with rocks! So weird and so uncool!" Kelly said.

"Annie is weird!" shouted Kelly, who is Rose's classmate.

Rose was hurt by their words to Annie, but she did not let them get to her. Rose reassured Annie. Rose told her how amazing crystals were. And she did not want to be like other kids who didn't understand about crystals.

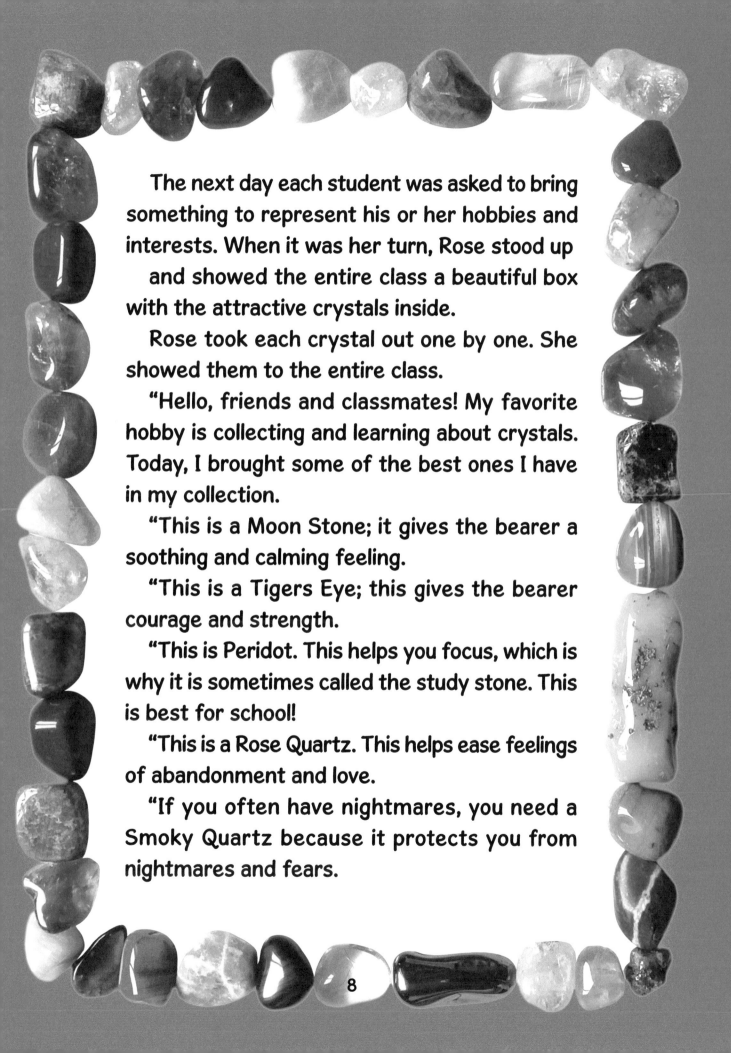

The next day each student was asked to bring something to represent his or her hobbies and interests. When it was her turn, Rose stood up and showed the entire class a beautiful box with the attractive crystals inside.

Rose took each crystal out one by one. She showed them to the entire class.

"Hello, friends and classmates! My favorite hobby is collecting and learning about crystals. Today, I brought some of the best ones I have in my collection.

"This is a Moon Stone; it gives the bearer a soothing and calming feeling.

"This is a Tigers Eye; this gives the bearer courage and strength.

"This is Peridot. This helps you focus, which is why it is sometimes called the study stone. This is best for school!

"This is a Rose Quartz. This helps ease feelings of abandonment and love.

"If you often have nightmares, you need a Smoky Quartz because it protects you from nightmares and fears.

9

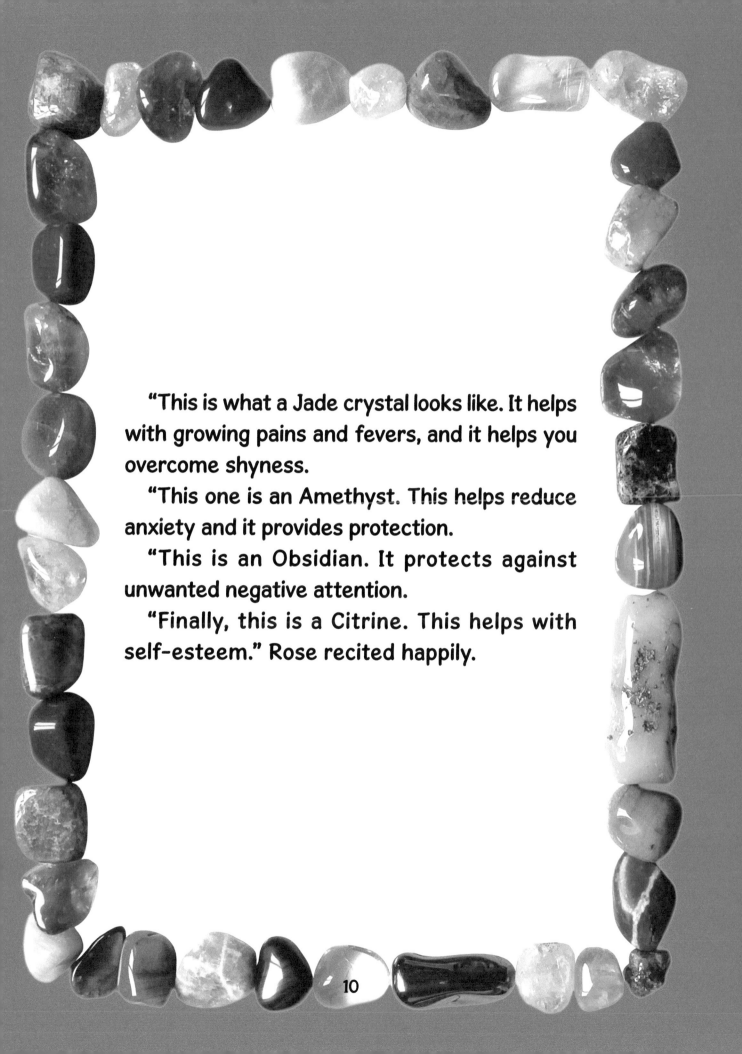

"This is what a Jade crystal looks like. It helps with growing pains and fevers, and it helps you overcome shyness.

"This one is an Amethyst. This helps reduce anxiety and it provides protection.

"This is an Obsidian. It protects against unwanted negative attention.

"Finally, this is a Citrine. This helps with self-esteem." Rose recited happily.

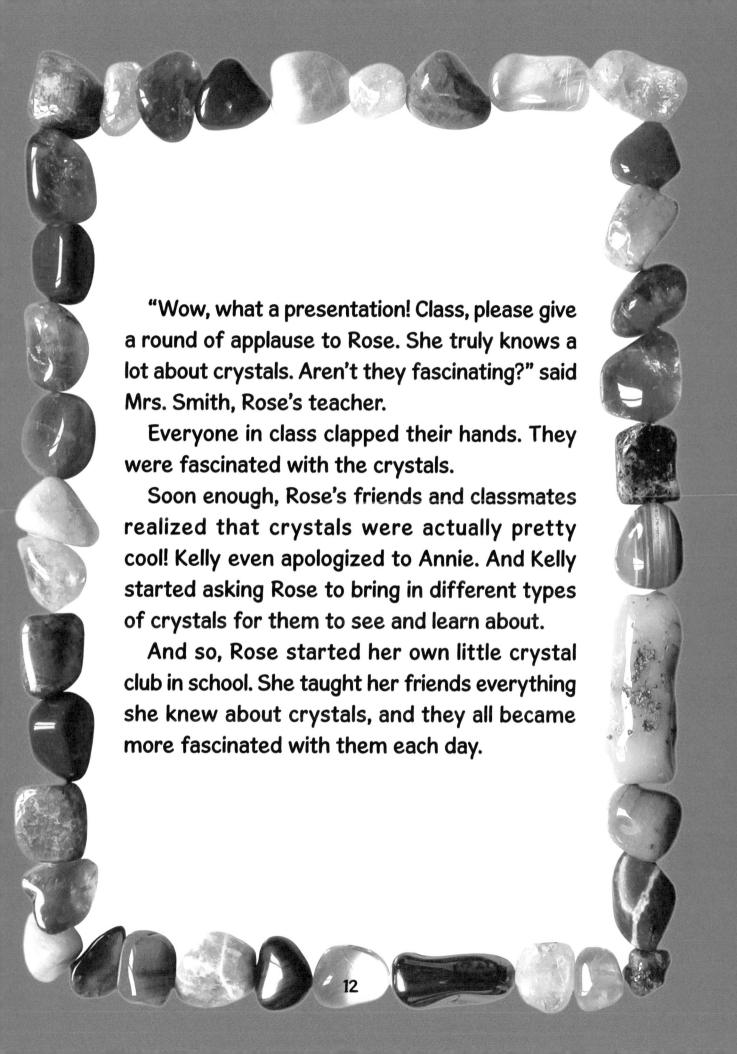

"Wow, what a presentation! Class, please give a round of applause to Rose. She truly knows a lot about crystals. Aren't they fascinating?" said Mrs. Smith, Rose's teacher.

Everyone in class clapped their hands. They were fascinated with the crystals.

Soon enough, Rose's friends and classmates realized that crystals were actually pretty cool! Kelly even apologized to Annie. And Kelly started asking Rose to bring in different types of crystals for them to see and learn about.

And so, Rose started her own little crystal club in school. She taught her friends everything she knew about crystals, and they all became more fascinated with them each day.

13

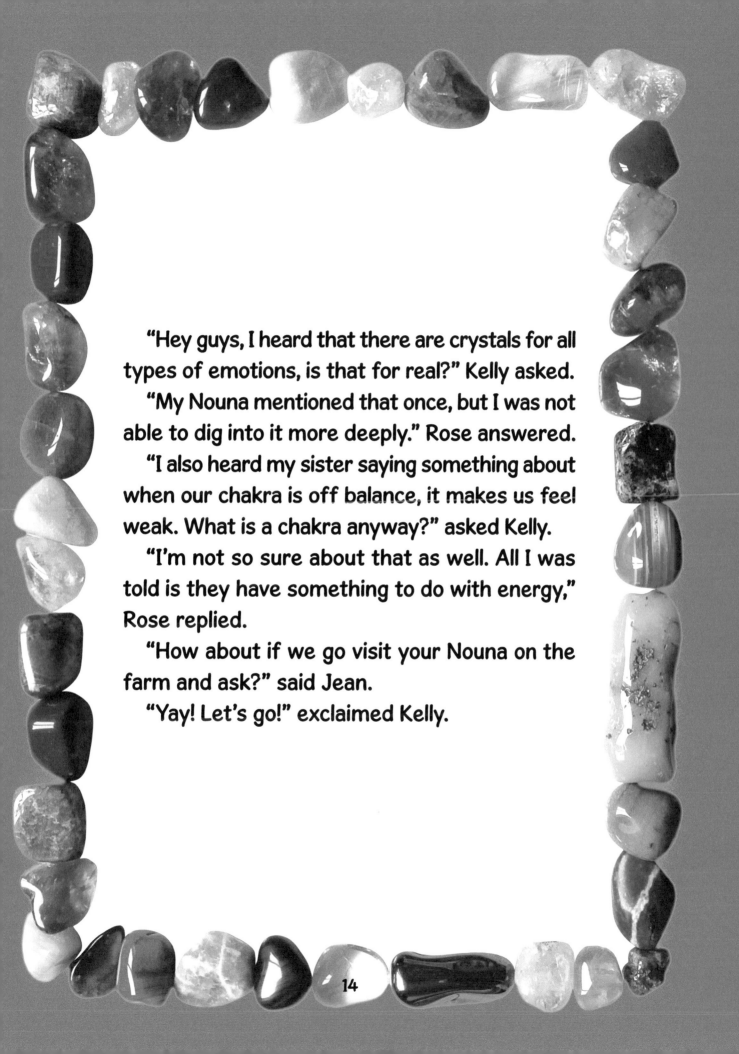

"Hey guys, I heard that there are crystals for all types of emotions, is that for real?" Kelly asked.

"My Nouna mentioned that once, but I was not able to dig into it more deeply." Rose answered.

"I also heard my sister saying something about when our chakra is off balance, it makes us feel weak. What is a chakra anyway?" asked Kelly.

"I'm not so sure about that as well. All I was told is they have something to do with energy," Rose replied.

"How about if we go visit your Nouna on the farm and ask?" said Jean.

"Yay! Let's go!" exclaimed Kelly.

15

"Hi girls! It's good to have all of you here today!" exclaimed Nouna.

"Hello Nouna! We want to ask you more questions about crystals. Is that OK? Rose asked.

"Certainly, I love talking about crystals because they are fun to have and collect. The first crystal I want to talk about is the Root crystal. The ones I have here are in colors red, garnet, and bloodstone. In general, red stones and crystals are associated with the Root Chakra. It's found in your tailbone area," Nouna explained.

"We were just talking about chakras. We do not understand it though. Can you explain it to us please? asked Kelly.

Nouna replied, "Chakras are energy points in your body. They run along your spine. Do you notice when you sometimes feel weak or sick for no reason? This means your energy sources are not balanced. You have to stay balanced often because it's our foundation. We feel relaxed, refreshed with a great sense of over all- well- being when our chakras are aligned and balanced. Sorry girls! I have some horses to feed. Talk to you next time, OK?"

"Thank you, Nouna," said the girls.

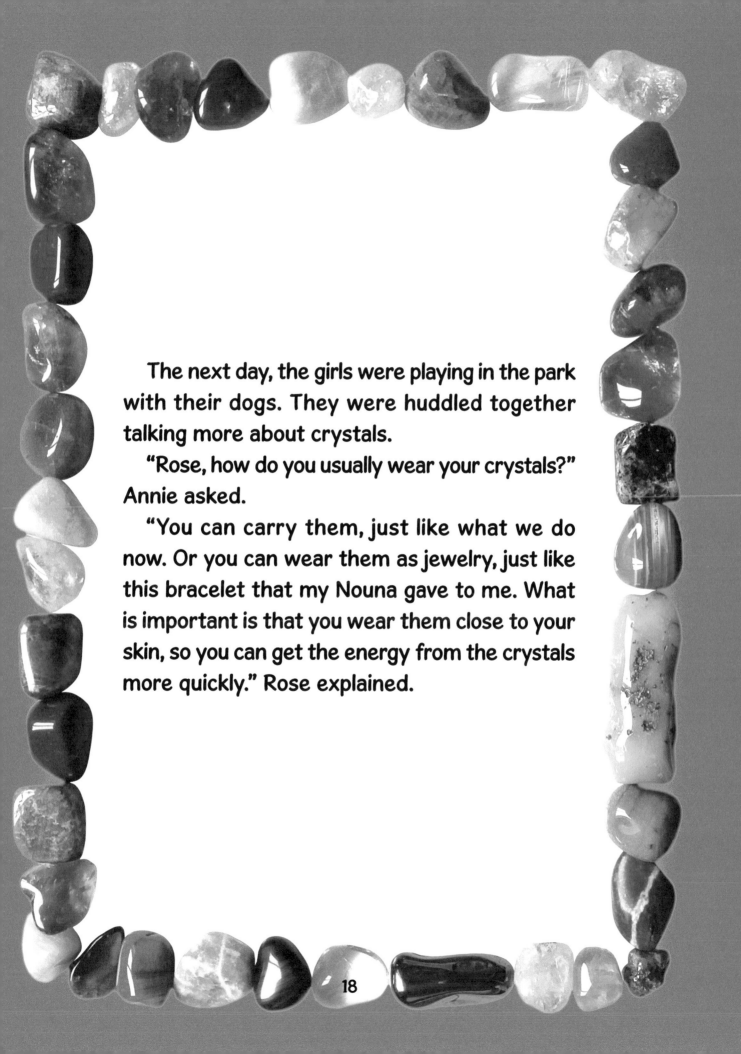

The next day, the girls were playing in the park with their dogs. They were huddled together talking more about crystals.

"Rose, how do you usually wear your crystals?" Annie asked.

"You can carry them, just like what we do now. Or you can wear them as jewelry, just like this bracelet that my Nouna gave to me. What is important is that you wear them close to your skin, so you can get the energy from the crystals more quickly." Rose explained.

From then on, Rose continued to teach her friends about crystals. She had found friends who appreciated and respected her love for crystals. And she continued to share her knowledge and passion for crystals with others because she knew everyone can benefit from their amazing powers.

The End.

Printed in the United States
by Baker & Taylor Publisher Services